MASTERING NFTS

THE COMPLETE GUIDE TO UNDERSTANDING AND WORKING WITH NFTS

By

JACKSON CARTER

Copyright © 2021

TABLE OF CONTENTS

Legal Notes

Mastering NFTs is meant for entertainment and educational use only. The information contained in this book is not intended as, and shall not be understood or construed as, financial advice.

Broad Base Publishing is not an attorney, accountant or financial advicsor, nor are we holding ourselves out to be, and the information contained in this book is not a substitute for financial advice from a professional who is aware of the facts and circumstances of your situation.

All attempts have been made to present factual information in an unbiased context. Please do your own research and do not enter into any financial situation without consulting with a professional.

WHAT IS AN NFT?

In today's increasingly tech-based society, it can be difficult to keep up with the latest information and technology-based opportunities that already exist. However, with so much technology available in the form of smartphones and Wi-Fi almost anywhere, the barriers between normal, everyday people and the various opportunities available are diminishing. In fact, it wasn't too long ago that the stock market had its own share of craziness due to this fact. The stock market phenomenon that was the Game Stop trading boom is not the only way that technology is becoming more helpful for everyday people to immerse themselves in areas that they've had limited access to before—everything from small businesses on Etsy blossoming during the pandemic to the ability to buy just about anything from around the world with just a few clicks. And with more and more people becoming tech-savvy or at least capable of figuring things out, it is no wonder that there have been a number of new trends going around that are solely based on the digital world.

From buzzwords like digital currency, mining, and Bitcoin, it can be very confusing to understand exactly how the world of digital purchasing works. For most people, the idea of buying something that you can't actually hold has actually been around for quite some time. Whether digitally downloading games or sending e-cards to people with silly animated pictures of your friends on the cover, the idea of paying real money for things that are completely digital isn't exactly a new concept. Plus, with social media and the ability to share things around the world in just seconds, there are tons of memes, gifs, and photos that have been shared, viewed and clicked on billions of times in their time of existence. However, all these things required that you paid for them with cash or credit and that you were just one of many who did so.

Even Bitcoin, which has become one of the biggest digitally traded items, is not exactly unique to you. This is called a fungible token. When you buy Bitcoin, no matter what the value is at the time of purchase, it is similar to exchanging money. Each Bitcoin, like dollar bills or coins, can be exchanged with each other because they have similar value. Additionally, just like dollar bills, Bitcoin and other fungible tokens can be broken up into smaller pieces and sold that way, such as coins for traditional currency or Satoshi for Bitcoin.

However, a new type of digital asset has become popular lately: non-fungible tokens (NFTs). Where fungible tokens, like Bitcoin, can be exchanged without really knowing one from another except for the value, non-fungible tokens are specifically recorded with information about not only its uniqueness, such as the first edition of a piece of digital art, but it is also something that an owner can prove that they own as that information is also included in the NFT. This BlockChain technology is basically what Bitcoin cryptocurrency is based on, but this new addition of using Ethereum is making this a very specific market with a lot of very different opportunities for NFTs. Instead of purchasing just a portion of the BlockChain, which is just like the rest of the other pieces that other people own, the NFTs add more information to the BlockChain, making each one specific and unique. This also makes them traceable and identifiable. It also means that they are exchangeable as not just currency but as a specific piece of digital property that you own. And this digital property has started taking many different forms.

While this small change of information coded into the NFT may seem small, it is actually opening up a huge market for tradeable goods that are strictly digital. Now, artists who work in the digital medium are able to not only sell their art as prints, they can also actually sell a limited amount of them to increase the uniqueness and rarity of their art. This also means that people who collect art or who are interested in rare objects can now expand their collection from physical items and also look into digital work, something that would have seemed like a waste of money before the ability to track ownership and uniqueness like never before.

This has created a frenzy of purchasing like never before with strictly digital artwork or even unique graphics that resemble 8-bit video game types of images. Some notable figures like Elon Musk are even selling their tweets or other opportunities to people who are willing to pay for them. They can be sure that they will not only receive confirmation that they have purchased these digital "goods" but can also be sure that they are not being conned into purchasing something that only looks unique but actually isn't. This security of knowing what you are getting and who has it, especially since the ledger is public and you can look up the actual owners of different NFTs, takes a lot of the risk out of purchasing NFTs unlike finding collectibles in a physical form that may end up being a counterfeit.

While anything can become an NFT, in order for it to draw attention and to do well, it, like all commodities, must be in demand. This means that there are a number of things that can be created as an NFT, such as pieces of art, tradeable icons, memes, tweets, digital collectibles like posters or virtual props from movie franchises, and many more others. However, not all of them will become as popular as others. Needless to say, many of them will not be anywhere close to being high in demand. Still, it is an exciting new market, with many looking to hoard and store these digital goods, assured of their rarity through this new technology and hoping that they will have a head start in this new opportunity.

Another thing that makes NFTs even more valuable is that they, unlike fungible tokens, cannot be split or shared. For example, two buyers cannot "share" a painting they purchased as an NFT, making this something that gives a true ownership feel. Artists or creators can, however, create and offer multiple versions of the same piece of work, each one marked with the number of which copy it is with a known quantity of how many are available. For example, the value of the first copy of a painting versus the 9,342nd out of 10,000 can be very different. This allows collectors to not just have one of the 10,000 but to know and attach extra value to the earliest created copies of it. This follows in the footsteps of physical goods. For example, think about Pokémon cards and the rarity of the first generation characters versus newer ones, or even back to the '90s with the Beanie Baby craze, with each of the actual stuffed animals coming in a variety of batch numbers, making some more exclusive and valuable than the more common ones.

WHAT ARE THE DIFFERENT TYPES OF NFT'S?

For those that are looking to get into the NFT market, there are a few differences between NFTs and other types of cryptocurrencies. One such difference is that NFTs are not traded on the markets and exchanges where other cryptocurrencies are traded. New, specialized markets like OpenBazaar are available for those looking to buy or sell NFTs instead. Additionally, NFTs are based on Ethereum, which is a cryptocurrency on its own. As part of the Ethereum BlockChain, the NFTs not only take up space on that BlockChain for the actual asset, but they are linked with additional information like a description, rarity, owner's name, etc. This means that you won't be able to use your other cryptocurrencies, like Bitcoin, to trade or purchase NFTs. It is a completely different series of steps to get involved in NFTs and requires buyers and traders to be ready to do some of the research behind getting involved, most of which is covered in the following chapter.

For many, it is a difficult concept to wrap their head around and the idea that digital work, even things like memes or tweets, could be sold and "owned" like never before. However, in the digital world that we find ourselves in, there are a number of people who are already ready to embrace the newness of NFTs. In fact, there are a number of businesses that have jumped on board or have been created just to deal with NFT purchasing, trading, and collection.

One of the newly launched sites is called Crypto Buds. It houses a collection of NFTs that was designed by a group of experienced artists, and each of the purchasable cards falls into a different category, ranging from DJ Headphones to Ear Buds to Gold-patterned. Each of these traits makes up the rareness of the card and helps to make up its value. They have created a system that randomizes buying options so that buyers are not just able to purchase whatever card they want at any time they want. Instead, they will be releasing the cards at different times, adding to the fervor and the feeling of scarcity, as you aren't really sure when the rarest cards may come up. Additionally, they even have a card that is designated as "Special," which is a one-of-a-kind card that is the most unique, rare, and valuable. Buyers are already flocking to pick up their own Crypto Buds and make sure that they get a piece of the action in the NFT market. They even have plans to roll out additional collections in the future so that even when all of the first cards are sold out, buyers can come back for more later on.

Another company riding the NFT wave is Terra Virtua. This site allows you to create a digital "Fan cave" where you can store and interact with all your NFT purchases. For example, you can even add your digital artwork to your room and then customize it with your favorite digital merchandise. They also release their own digitized merchandise based on movie franchises or pop culture that you can purchase from them to add to your fan cave. Similar to those who display their artwork or rare collectibles in cases in their own homes, now anyone can access their collectibles from the internet and show them off during a lunch date or a short hop on the subway. This also means that buyers don't have to worry about the security and physical space that would be required if they bought a lot of collectibles, such as copies of every single Harry Potter film's movie posters. Now, they can simply purchase the digital versions and never have to stress about their upkeep or maintenance.

However, selling digital goods is just the beginning of NFT possibilities. Although it is not yet widely used, NFTs could also be used as digital money to buy physical goods. This may seem counterintuitive, but the digital, traceable, verifiable ownership that comes with an NFT can be just as commonly used and expected when purchasing lands, having deeds, or other paperwork, licenses, or certificates. By using NFTs as a security token for real-world assets, the world could see a drastic change in the way that information, ownership, and value are dispersed among items. This could mean that you would have virtual access anywhere with internet in order to show proof of ownership or to access information. Additionally, this would make it hard for certain credentials or things to be forged because the purchaser's information and the specific information for the asset they are claiming to own will not be included in the NFT.

How To Sell Your Artwork With NFT's

Because of the flexible nature of NFTs, it is no wonder that many in the art community are now finding a new way to make money off of their digital pieces. Whereas before, people might buy prints of a digital work online or even from limited pieces the artist produced themselves, allowing the artist to limit production and reproduction of a piece in order to create exclusivity and rarity—this is something new for a lot of digital artists. For many years, digital art often meant doing a lot of the selling process on your own or building up a portfolio for an animation job or something similar. Now, artists are able to find new ways to use their pieces and even replace the traditional job setting by continuing to make artworks and selling them as NFTs instead.

In the early part of 2021, NFTs have become a new set of hot commodities, not only making the news in the tech community but also in the art community. In March 2021, one artist, Mike Winklemann, known as Beeple in the art community, had a collage of his digital artwork up for auction at Christie's, one of the prestigious art houses in the world. Not only did he sell his artwork, which he did not intend to do with his portfolio as a graphic designer, but he also did so in a huge way. With a large social media following of almost two million, Beeple was a known artist, but wasn't the type to have his work displayed in galleries or sold at large auction houses. So, this was something completely new and exciting for him and the art community as a whole. This was definitely a headline-making event as the market proved that not only are NFTs collectible but that they are also worth as much as many of the most famous art pieces in history.

For Beeple, this wasn't just a piece that he created with selling it as an NFT in mind. He worked on the various pieces that made up the 5,000-image collage, "Everydays: The First 5000 Days" over the course of 13 years. The auction began with an opening bid of only $100, but over the course of the bidding, an astounding 350 people chimed in and the price went up tremendously. In the end, the work, which he shared had taken him years to create all of the pieces and then compile them to form this collage, sold for an outstanding $69.3 million. This sale put Beeple up there with some of the most expensive artists still alive; up there with David Hockney and Jeff Koons.

And he is not the only one to see huge profits from his digital works via NFTs. A teenage artist known as FEWOCiOUS sold a piece for tens of thousands of dollars on his birthday. A group of 16,000 pieces of NFT-based art known as Hashmasks sold for $9 million in February 2020. Additionally, a card featuring soccer player, Kylian Mbappe, sold for almost $65,000. Clearly, NFT art is becoming a much more commonplace thing in the art community, even if the pieces themselves are anything but common.

With decades of art being created digitally by both professionals, amateurs, and everyone in between, it was never something that could make a lot of money in the collectibles market because of the lack of opportunity to feel like you had something unique. However, like Beeple, many are beginning to see the opportunities in not just selling their artwork but doing so as an NFT to increase collectability and interest as well as price.

For those interested in creating their own digital artwork or other types of NFTs, the process may seem daunting. Especially with a lot of jargon and very specific methods for selling NFTs, it can be hard to imagine going through the process in order to get your work out there. However, it isn't that difficult once you learn the process and become familiar with how NFTs work and are sold. One of the first things to understand is that you will need to set up a crypto wallet and become familiar with the Ethereum costs associated with selling and buying any NFT.

The crypto wallet is where you can set up an account and link it to your sales or purchases. Here, you can store your Ethereum and also receive it when you make sales. There are a lot of different options for crypto wallets. Some of the biggest ones include MetaMask, TrustWallet, Argent, and Coinbase. MetaMask even opened the door to making your crypto wallet and specifically managing your NFTs an option while on the go with their app. The good thing about Ethereum is that you can store it on various wallets, not just one or two, making it flexible and something you can tailor to your specific needs. There are two specific things you need to find and remember or write down for your crypto wallet: the seed phrase and your wallet address.

In case you lose access to your wallet either by forgetting your password or you are locked out, the seed phrase is what will allow you to get access back into your NFTs. There is nothing worse than being locked out of your own money and purchases, so make sure that you write down your seed wallet and back it up in multiple places. Some even suggest that you should not use cloud-based systems to store this info or share it with anyone so that you are completely sure of the security of your investments. Additionally, your wallet address is where others will send money when they want to purchase something from you. Similar to a banking account and routing number, you will need this to get paid, so make sure to find it and save it so that you can link it to your collection when you are ready to sell.

Once your wallet has been set up, you can go ahead and purchase some Ethereum (ETH). This is the currency used to purchase part of an Ethereum BlockChain in order to create an NFT, and most places will show you the conversion to dollars, or any other currency you are using. However, just like gold or silver, the price of Ethereum changes over time, similar to the stock market's fluctuations. At the time of writing, one ETH is equivalent to $1572.92. This will help you determine what you can afford and how much ETH you need to make a purchase, as well as the prices you want to set your artwork at.

Ensure that you purchase more ETH than you need due to gas fees. Gas fees are transaction costs you have to pay in order to buy ETH. They, too, fluctuate depending on the supply and demand of the Ethereum BlockChain. You may want to do some research about current gas fees and know that no matter the marketplace through which you choose to sell your artwork, they do not control the gas fees; they are beholden to the market just like you are. Similarly, there may be a fee associated with just posting your work on a specific marketplace. So be sure to purchase enough ETH in order to complete your transactions and list your pieces.

Next, you'll need to select the marketplace you want to use in order to sell your pieces. Some, like Nifty Gateway, MakersPlace, OpenSea, and Decentraland, have a variety of options for you to work with and may have a lot of different styles they focus on. This means that you have to do your own research and see which ones fit the bill. You should look into the ease of finding artwork, how they are ranked or presented to potential buyers, fees, how they assign NFTs, or if your art would be a good fit for this marketplace's customers. Additionally, if you are more interested in very specific avenues of selling, there are places like NBA Top Shot that sell specific clips and "moments" from NBA history for you to collect. There may be a marketplace out there, like NBA Top Shot, that focuses specifically on the niche you like, so make sure to explore those options as well.

Once you've decided on a marketplace, you must sign up and put all your information in order. This will include your crypto wallet and wallet address as well as paying for your fees or gas fees in order to create listings. Then, you can begin to set up your collection. Essentially, your collection is like your private gallery for your work, which you want to display through your chosen marketplace. Customers can find you or your artwork through the various search options in the marketplace or through sale rankings or changes. Through this, they may click on your collection to see what other pieces you have available for sale or to check prices and compare to past works you've sold or a similar piece they are eyeing.

For this reason, you want to make sure that you do whatever you can to set up your collection to really represent your work and your brand. This may mean adding a banner image of you or your art, adding specific descriptions in your allotted spaces on the page, or even organizing your pieces the way you want them to be displayed to a potential customer. Similar to an actual physical gallery, think about the experience you want to give a customer when they enter your collection. Depending on your style and goals, you can personalize a lot of what they will see, which will make you stand out from the crowd and make them even more interested or excited about your art.

As you get ready to list your first item, it is usually a good idea to check out the platform and marketplace in order to see what is working for other artists. This could mean simply going through your options as a seller, setting the commission rates you will make from both primary sales and secondary ones, choosing currencies and social tokens you accept, and figuring out how to list and customize your pieces. This could also mean checking out other successful artists' collections and taking note of which pieces or themes are doing well and comparing them to what you have that may fill that category, or even just looking at the descriptions and information about other pieces as well to get a feel for what buyers will expect to see from your collection.

Once you are set up, it is time to add your art. In some marketplaces, you can even collaborate with other artists and create a joint collection, each of you adding your own pieces and making commissions from them separately. However, once you are ready to upload your art, the process is fairly self-explanatory on many of the marketplaces' interfaces. You will upload your piece to the site, set the price and description, and the marketplace will translate that into your NFT information and charge you a gas fee for purchasing a bit of the BlockChain for this piece. However, there are ways you can avoid this fee until you make your first sale, so be sure to read through the various marketplace options before deciding on one.

When uploading your art, you also have to set the available quantity. Because of the nature of NFTs, this will be a set number that collectors can use to determine the scarcity and value of a piece compared to other pieces. For example, a piece that only has three copies made versus one that has 10,000 made will have a different value in the eyes of collectors and you may be able to capitalize on that in order to make more profits. However, there is still value in larger quantities of popular pieces, which will allow you to make more, steady sales instead of sporadic large ones. Additionally, some marketplaces may not allow you to adjust the quantity as you upload your piece; they may require you to add each copy or edition of your art as a new listing, meaning that there may be a lot more fees or in the very least, it will be a much more time-consuming process than in other marketplaces.

Once your art is listed, it is time to bring in customers to your collection. While marketplaces have natural traffic, it can be hard to gain traction as a newcomer in a rapidly growing marketplace. Some buyers will only check the top-ranked artists or the trending pieces, while others may look for things more specific, or just want to look at new artists or pieces. The important thing is to try and drum up organic sales in the meantime so that you can build up not only your wallet but also your reputation and profile on the marketplace. This may mean turning to social media as a way to spread information about your pieces being available. But be wary. There have been a few cases of artists trying to share their pieces on social media only to have others use an image of that post as their own NFT, basically using your artwork and words as a way to make money without creating it themselves. However, there is a lot to be said for bringing in a few customers, friends, family, or others who can help you begin your NFT career.

Additionally, you can reach out to other artists on social media or through the marketplace and network with them. You can form collaborative groups or work on pieces together to mutually benefit you both by drawing attention and customers to both your collections. Look for ways to help spread the word about your art in order to get the ball rolling. Some marketplaces, like Rarible, even have tokens you can earn as a creator just by actively participating on their platform, which is another way you can interact with potential customers and get your collection into more digital hands.

GET STARTED WITH NFT TODAY

For an easy way to get started head over to StartOpenSeas.com to start trading on the web's largest and easiest to use NFT Trading Market.

*The website above contains an affiliate link, which may lead to a payout that will help support our small publishing company at no cost to you.

CRYPTOPUNKS

There are also NFTs that aren't actually created by a person, which are selling for a lot of money as well. One of the first-ever NFT was released back in 2017 by a two-person company called Larva Labs. This company created the project CryptoPunks, which sold out pretty quickly. One of the most interesting things about NFTs is that they are not like purchasing copyright, the type many large companies or businesses have over specific logos or catchphrases. Instead, by using the NFT system, every single piece is literally owned by a buyer, and while there are copies out there, as there are with many of the things that get published on the Internet these days, you as the owner know that you actually own the original, making this market even more interesting when it comes to collectibles like the CryptoPunks project.

This project generated a limited amount of 10,000 24x24 pixel art images that resemble the 8-bit images from early computer games, featuring faces and different features, many of them fitting their "punk" name. Each visual token was created using a computer algorithm and a set number of attributes that could be assigned to each one, varying from zero attributes to seven. Depending on the combination of attributes, each image was specific and individual. Although there may be many CryptoPunks that feature a mustache or 3D glasses, the combination of a CryptoPunk with a mustache, 3D glasses, red hair, and a gold chain will be a specific and completely uncopied version.

Other attributes range from the type of Punk you have purchased such as alien, ape, zombie, female, or male, and a few limited unattributed punks that are simply bald and have basic facial features. These specific unattributed Punks number only eight out of the total 10,000, making them one of the more rare purchases you could find. Currently, however, there are none being offered for sale by their owners. And they are all currently owned, all 10,000 of them.

The interesting part is that when Larva Labs decided to release the CryptoPunks, they were really experimenting with something new and decided that although they had created the basic attributes and used the algorithm to create the unique images, they didn't know what kind of response they would get from the public. Because of this and the newness of NFTs, they decided to go ahead and release their project for free. What the initial buyers needed to do was to cover the small gas fees that were associated with the transaction and they could scoop up a number of these interesting, unique images for themselves. Because of the nature of NFTs, when they released the CryptoPunks to the BlockChain, the information became permanently written there, unable to be modified by anyone, making it impossible to change the identity of each Punk, as well as replicate or steal it. This, along with the interesting form that NFTs can take, make many investors feel more secure and trustful of the emerging marketplaces.

As one of the first-ever collectible NFTs, CryptoPunks definitely set a tone for the market. While Larva Labs did some work to reach out to people in forums and other places to spread the word, people didn't show a lot of interest the first day it was released, even though they were essentially free. The two men behind Larva Labs were unsure whether their idea and project would ever materialize the way they had imagined it could. However, their project was picked up by Mashable and an article was written focusing on CryptoPunks. Overnight, they went from selling only 20 or 30 CryptoPunks on Friday to completely selling all the 10,000 by Saturday morning.

It didn't take long after that for the secondary marketplace to crop up and others started offering their almost free CryptoPunks for sale by that Saturday afternoon. The first sale from one owner to another happened that afternoon for a total of 10 ETH, equal to about $3,500 at the time. Obviously, with some of them now selling for over $20,000, the market is still going strong today. And not all of them are worth the same amount, just like any collector would expect. Needless to say, the men behind the project were astounded at the rapid turnaround and the way the whole project had taken off and launched NFTs into the public eye.

Just like physical items that are collectible, such as coins, cards, or art, there are specific features that make the Punks worth a certain amount of Ethereum. While the number of attributes is definitely one of them, with the rarest being a single Punk with a maximum of seven attributes available, there is a variety of Punks that are currently offered at any given time by their owners for purchase. It will never be more than they currently are now. This creates a digital rarity of these pieces of BlockChain that have been imprinted with these images, which depends on how many there are that share certain attributes, or how the number of attributes helps sellers determine how much their specific Punks are worth. Additionally, each Punk is given its own profile page so that you can see just what makes it unique and special, identifying its given attributes and whether it is up for sale or currently being held by its owner.

For example, for stringy-haired Punks, there are a total of 463 that were created and owned. Of those 463, only 53 are currently being offered by their owners. They are selling for an average of 14.97 ETH in that category, but the cheapest available at the moment is priced at 21.2 ETH. Other attributes such as Punks with welding goggle attribute are only 86 in number, with 15 available for sale. To many collectors, they are worth more since there are fewer of them available. The average price for the welding goggles punks, regardless of their other attributes, is 44 ETH, with the cheapest one on the market right now listed at 58.89ETH. The rarest attribute is the beanie, which adds a red, blue, and yellow propeller-style beanie to the top of each of the 44 Punks in that category. While there are ten available, the average price of beanie Punks is 81.82ETH and the cheapest one for sale at the moment is

269.99ETH, meaning that the cheapest beanie Punk is worth a whopping $435,358.88 using the current exchange rate.

They have even come up with a great way of showing you the Punks that are available in a visual format. While the list options are available on the CryptoPunks site, where you can identify which attributes you're looking for, you can also browse visually. There is a composite image of every single Punk that has a color code, which can help potential buyers determine the status of a Punk on sight. Blue backgrounds mean that the owner is not offering that claimed Punk for sale at the moment. Red backgrounds mean that the Punk is currently available for purchase or bid. Purple backgrounds mean that there is an active bid on the Punk and you can click on it to learn more about it. This is an interesting format because it allows buyers to find the attributes they are interested in purchasing, not just based on a single attribute or two.

While the concept of pixel punk art may not seem very appealing to some people, investors and those looking to join the fray of the digital currency world are definitely interested. Over the past twelve months, there have been over 7,500 sales of CryptoPunks. The average selling price for that same timeframe is 14.82ETH, or about $12,171. Over the course of the lifetime of the project, since 2017, the total value of all their sales is 111.56K ETH, which is about $204.52 million. And all this happened with the initial sales being free, except for a small ETH gas fee. This goes to show that not only are NFTs like CryptoPunks a hot commodity but that they can also be a great investment for those looking to get into the cryptocurrency world or even start off their digital collection journey. As one of the very first NFTs on the market, CryptoPunks have significant historical value as collectors are excited to own one of the first products of this emerging marketplace.

For those who are used to buying digital goods, for example, the craze for the latest skins in the Fortnite game that many people are excited about every time the Epic Games crew releases a new season or character, it can be hard to see why having a CryptoPunk or another NFT would be worth so much. While skins and other digital downloads range from free to over $50, there aren't really many that are worth tens of thousands. However, when examining the basic differences between digital downloads like skins and NFTs, you have to remember that while you may "own" a skin in your inventory and can use it at will in the game, you can't sell it to anyone else or trade it. Oftentimes, you aren't even the only one in your lobby wearing that skin as well since hundreds and thousands of copies of the same thing can be bought in just a few hours.

However, NFTs like CryptoPunks are unique. Yes, their copies can be made available but only one person owns the original, unlike the skins in a video game. While an NFT can be used and interacted with in some ways, such as creating a fan cave full of your NFTs or purchasing memes or gifs to share with others, when you purchase one as an NFT, you can be sure that you are the clear owner, written into the BlockChain for anyone to verify as needed. Additionally, even when skins or other digital downloads are retired or are no longer supported by the servers they are on, NFTs are secure and will continue to exist as yours, making this an investment that you can count on in the long run, not depending on a third-party source to control what you've spent all that money on.

Moon Cats

With the emergence of CryptoPunks and a new type of collectible market available, it was only a matter of time before other companies emerged and released their own sets of collectibles. However, as there are now more and more companies jumping on the NFT bandwagon, the rarity and desirability of the newer, more mass-produced collectibles have become much lower compared to the CryptoPunk frenzy.

As a result, there are people out there looking to dig through the past and find any of the long lost NFTs from back when CryptoPunks started out in the hopes of finding a few historical collectibles that will, hypothetically, be more valuable over time due to their age and history before the more mainstream NFTs became available. And just a few weeks ago, it seemed that digital archeologists digging back into the NFT annals had made a truly rare discovery.

In August 2017, Ponderware, a company made up of two developers, created their own NFTs and wrote them into the BlockChain. This date makes their project, MoonCatRescue, the second oldest NFT, only younger than CryptoPunks. However, it seemed like nobody had really heard of them until a tweet went out asking if anyone knew about them and how old they were. However, the tweet also detailed part of the reason MoonCatRescue might not have been heard of by many people: there was a problem with the coding.

The whole project focused on the idea that buyers would search for MoonCats and bring their favorites to the BlockChain, with a limit of 25,600. This meant that they could create endless supplies of MoonCats, but only a certain number could become contracted NFTs. The concept was that buyers could rescue these cats from the moon and bring them to earth through the transaction, and they would then own them as an NFT. They could also collect variations or different types of cats. Like CryptoPunks, they were essentially free when they were released and only needed a small gas fee to own the ones brought to the BlockChain. Not only was this a great niche for collectors and those who love cats to invest in a cute mission to rescue the digital cats, but MoonCats would also allow owners to give their MoonCats their own, permanent names, a type of customization that was completely new to the market as they allowed the MoonCats to be written into the BlockChain after the owner "found" or generated them.

However, the company was also planning to offer a monetized version of specialty cats, the Genesis Cats, which would be comprised of just 256 black and white MoonCats that didn't have to be "found" and brought over; they would be available for sale in small increments over a certain period of time until they were all collected. But things didn't work out that way after the initial release; there was a problem with the program and a bug prevented Ponderware from accessing the funds that would be used for the transactions. After this, the site went dark. And without anything really happening, they were out of the conversation. Just a few months later, a new NFT called CryptoCats launched and seemed to do well where MoonCats had been unable to capitalize.

Then for the next few years, other NFTs became popular and MoonCatRescue became a thing that only a few had seen and most had never even heard of. It wasn't until the recent tweet asking about the age of the NFT, which could be viewed through the parts they had written into the BlockChain back in 2017, that people were off to the races to rescue some MoonCats. The tweet, though, did caution that the coding of the original site was broken and that those who wished to buy MoonCats would have to work around the system and take a few additional steps in order to "fix" it so that they could truly be collected.

Others jumped on board as well and they started sharing the steps and information to those looking to purchase MoonCats. As with many other digital fields, the cryptocurrency field of NFTs was rife with programmers and tech-savvy people who could figure out how to make things like MoonCats work despite the fact that their coding was outdated and "broken."

Now, in order to rescue the MoonCats, a buyer would need to find or generate a MoonCat using the provided web address on the website. Then, they would need to record the seed and ID of the cat that they generated and pay the gas fee, since they were still essentially free, in order to claim it as their own. Then, because of the outdated coding of the MoonCats, they would need to be "wrapped" in a different contract and listed on a marketplace and traded like a normal NFT.

Within just a few hours of the tweet—three actually—all 25,600 regular MoonCats had been rescued. They jumped from a gas fee of just cents to over $600,000 during that time, making their way to the top of the charts of Ethereum network fees raised by a specific NFT. Needless to say, it was a historic find for the digital world and probably one of the only digital archeological digs that had resulted in something interesting in the history of technology. Many were fanatically going after the MoonCats as not only a chance to own a piece of history but also to say that they had been a part of the resurgence of a long lost NFT project, many of them saying that this event would go down in history and many years from now maybe looked back upon as the first digital archeological opportunity.

While this was a recent happening, all of the MoonCats are owned and many of them are actively being traded. However, there is a huge discrepancy regarding what the MoonCats are worth, average prices being 1 ETH, but ranging from 0.2 ETH to 20 ETH depending on the type and the buyer. Still, it is a very specific piece of NFT history as MoonCats not only had a huge sales day, but they are also now out of the shadows and listed as the second true NFT ever created.

Developers even came out of the woodworks as the MoonCatRescue took off out of the blue once more. They even logged onto the site and their Twitter page and shared that they were currently trying to reconnect to the "moon base." Then in March 2021, they posted an update on their site that they were very excited that all the MoonCats have been rescued. They also shared that they would still be able to generate 160 more Genesis MoonCats if the community wanted them to. However, they also shared that if they did, there would be a high chance that bots would pick apart those 160 too quickly for anyone to truly get a shot at them. Plus, the bots would be paying exorbitant gas fees in order to beat regular buyers.

They decided to leave it to the community of those interested in MoonCats to vote on whether or not to pursue an option that would bring the Genesis MoonCats to fruition and find a way to beat the bots so that collectors would have an opportunity to get their hands on one of those rare black and white cats. They even offered voters a chance at a free rescue cat just for casting their vote. They were very transparent with the community and shared that they had blocked the voting system from their own addresses due to their conflict of interest so that they would be unable to vote on whether or not to recall the Genesis MoonCats. They wanted the community to know that they were truly asking for their opinion and valued it, knowing that they would continue to thrive no matter what everyone decided.

After the vote came to an end, it was decided that the community did not want the remaining Genesis MoonCats to be generated. The developers shared this on their site with an update and stayed true to their original development by sharing a story about the Genesis MoonCats. They shared that the community on the moon needed leaders and that the Genesis MoonCats made the decision to become those leaders for the MoonCat society. They also chose not to join us here on earth and would instead remain and thrive on the moon.

This essentially meant that although they released a total of 25,600 MoonCats, both regular and Genesis versions, they had only managed to generate and rescue 25,440 due to the final cats "staying behind." Still, this was a win for not only the MoonCatRescue developers but also for many collectors who now have the opportunity to own or trade a few interesting pieces of NFT history.

Although it took many more years than the original developers had intended, MoonCatRescue ended up getting a special place in the cryptocurrency world and once again drew attention to the NFT market as a whole. And it seems that the idea of MoonCats wasn't something that was going to fade away any time soon as CryptoCats and CryptoKitties have become large, successful NFTs as well.

CRYPTOKITTIES

While the MoonCatRescue project focused on the story of rescuing unique cats from their lunar homes and CryptoPunks were all about the algorithm-generated attributes that each NFT was assigned, new NFTs have been created with more than just purchasing and trading the NFT in mind. Now, there are even NFTs, like CryptoKitties, that allow buyers and collectors to interact with their NFTs in a new way as well as with other collectors without giving up their own NFT to do so.

Following quickly on the heels of both CryptoPunks and MoonCatRescue, CryptoKitties was created toward the end of 2017 and became very popular the following years. Now, the community is huge and thriving due to the various features they have created for their community to enjoy with their CryptoKitties. Within a week of the launch of CryptoKitties, not only had the site taken up 13% of Ethereum usage, but they also clogged up much of the market through their breeding exchanges, making it hard for other companies to gain much traction during that time.

Ever since their release, they've been able to stay on top of the NFT game and have a significant amount of banking behind the original development. With huge aspirations for the CryptoKitty collectible, both Andreesen Horowitz and Union Square Ventures spent $12 million investing in the original game's release. Their hope was to not only use it as a BlockChain application but to also help bring

Ethereum's BlockChain technology into the spotlight and make it mainstream for other applications. Things like real-world purchases, buying real estate, or even forming contracts between two parties that must meet certain requirements before the transaction may take place are all possible uses that the investors hope to see by backing CryptoKitties and helping to show the world what the NFT wave has to offer.

Similar to CryptoPunks, CryptoKitties has distinct features and they are valued-based, somewhat depending on which "cattributes" they have. Some are dressed in ninja garb and others have specific eye colors. Then, there are the traits and features that they have such as an impish grin or bloodshot eyes, some even sprouting wings or donning a floating crown over their heads. Recently, it was reported that the CryptoKitties site had reached out to NBA basketball star, Stephen Curry, to seek his help in designing and releasing the first-ever celebrity CryptoKitties to the market in the near future. This could open an opportunity for other NFTs to capitalize on celebrity endorsements and features to help boost their popularity and possibly truly launch NFTs into a widely accepted and used form of currency in the world.

However, unlike CryptoPunks or even MoonCats, CryptoKitties is given a specific genetic code that allows their traits to interact with other CryptoKitties through a breeding process that is very similar to the breeding that many animal handlers do. Not only does the site create a profile listing each CryptoKitties' cattributes, but they also share their lineage, showing pictures of their mother and father or any children they may have sired through the breeding process and what they look like based on the Sire and Dam that created them.

This process definitely adds another level to the NFT market since people will be able to not only purchase a unique token in the form of a digital cat but they can also interact with other collectors and choose to breed their own cats with others for a fee. This allows collectors to build up their own collection by trading with others, making ETH from breeding fees, and interacting with the community while still keeping their favorites. Additionally, the breeding system allows generations to be tracked so that earlier generations of cats become more valuable and have likely sired many of the other lines that are currently owned by newer buyers. Generations are also important as the new kitten will be one generation more than their highest generation parent. So for example, if a Gen 4 and a Gen 8 were to breed, their kitten would result in a Gen 9, making the lower generations of Kitties more valuable, especially those with interesting traits or attributes.

Plus, there is a timing system so that breeders are not able to breed kitten after kitten. Males have a cooldown time between breeding sessions, and the cooldown grows each time the male mates. Females, on the other hand, are unable to breed again while incubating a kitten, making the interactions feel very realistic and interesting as anticipation is built wondering how your new kitten will turn out. Will it have the father's yellow stripes and handlebar mustache, or will it take the mother's timid grin and distinct teal ears and tail? All of these things make CryptoKitties an interesting and immersive experience for collectors who are looking for something more than just a digital good to have in a crypto wallet.

Additionally, cat lovers of all kinds will get a chance to experience cat ownership and breeding. Now, they can even purchase forty CryptoKitties and not have to worry about feeding or housing them in real life, but can still experience some aspects of ownership that are enjoyable. For those with allergies, apartments, or just busy lives, CryptoKitties can be a fun and easy way to get a feel of a true pet without the responsibility of actually keeping one alive. The site also allows interactions with your cats and community in the form of puzzles and other activities that you can participate in once you become a CryptoKitty owner.

As far as value goes, each CryptoKitty, like each CryptoPunk, has a specific value attached to them based on their attributes. On the CryptoKitties site right now, the cheapest CryptoKitty is available for purchase at just .004 ETH or just $6.48. This kitty is named Fabio Goodthang and is a Gen 11 who hasn't bred at all yet. He features a cotton candy base fur color and emerald, green accents. He also has thick, fluffy Siberian-style fur. On the other hand, the most expensive is listed at 999+ ETH or over $999k. This cat is named Hup I of Flamandia 25 *'s Gen. Not only does he have gold eyes, an onyx base fur with chocolate highlights, but his environment or background is a sparkling rainbow. Clearly, there are many options available in between for collectors to peruse. And at a starting cost of just under $10 for the cheaper ones, just about anyone can become a CryptoKitty owner and see what it is like to own a digital cat, or twelve.

The FAQs section allows people to learn more about the CryptoKitties site and attributes, as well as how trading and breeding are done. For example, when breeding your CryptoKitty, you can unlock new things in their "DNA" that may show up in their children since they were recessive traits. This is similar to colored eyes cropping up after skipping generations in a dark-eyed family in real life. Additionally, by mating certain traits with each other, mutations can also be unlocked, making anyone capable of creating valuable and rare CryptoKitties depending on the breeding choices they make over time. And for those just getting started, the site even offers a Kitty Class, where they walk you through the breeding process with two sample cats so that you can get a handle on how the interactions work and what you need to do or look out for when you decide to breed your own cats.

Similarly, there are different varieties of cats available, such as Special Edition, Exclusive, and Fancy Cats. Some of these, such as Fancy Cats, are generated by special "recipes" of cattributes being bred together and can even result in a kitten with custom art like Hup I mentioned above. Collectors can begin to look up how past matches have ended up and trace certain attributes back all the way to the original breeding cats through the site, which can help them get an idea of how various interactions or mutations might happen in their own CryptoKitties when they decide to breed them. Exclusive Cats are the ones that are dropped in by the developers and often feature custom features that can never be replicated, making them very unique and rare. Similarly, Special Edition Cats are released on occasion and feature special traits, but are released in larger batches and with the ability to replicate the unique traits through breeding.

Also, there is a limit of 50,000 Gen 0 Kitties—the ones that are not created through breeding but instead dropped in by the developers every 15 minutes. This makes them very rare as well. And because of their generation number, they will have faster breeding times than those that are at a higher generation level. All of these factors affect the value of any given CryptoKitty and can help collectors determine how they would like to diversify their collection or whether they'd like to focus on a specific type or breed a specific cat to produce a certain attribute in its offspring.

Despite being one of the early NFTs, CryptoKitties has maintained a steady presence in the NFT marketplace. Not only are they collectible but they also offer a lot of customizations and choices for collectors to interact with, which help them to maintain their longevity as a popular

NFT option. Similarly, the low entry fee to own a CryptoKitty makes this an easy way to get your feet wet in the Ethereum market and requires virtually nothing in order to invest in your first NFT.

Although there is a low cost of entry, there are many options that are also good for Ethereum millionaires out there looking to add very rare pieces to their collections. Interestingly, the most expensive CryptoKitty was once listed at 600 ETH, worth $114,481.59 at the time, almost three times the value of the most expensive cat to exist in the physical world. Some reports even say that some exchanges were pushing the price toward the $300,000 mark. However, the average sale price is around $65 for most CryptoKitties. It seems that the idea of digital pet ownership isn't as crazy as it may sound.

The most important thing to remember about any sort of NFT, whether it is a digital piece of art or a virtual pet, is that NFTs fluctuate. The value of digital items, like physical ones, will change over time and it can be difficult, if not impossible, to predict by how much the value will change and how long before that change happens. Similar to the stock market or other opportunities to invest money in, ensuring that you have a keen eye, doing your own research, and staying on top of the market are all important tips to help you make the right investment decisions.

GET STARTED WITH NFT TODAY

For an easy way to get started head over to StartOpenSeas.com to start trading on the web's largest and easiest to use NFT Trading Market.

*The website above contains an affiliate link, which may lead to a payout that will help support our small publishing company at no cost to you.

MORE FROM JACKSON CARTER BIOGRAPHIES

My goal is to spark the love of reading in young adults around the world. Too often children grow up thinking they hate reading because they are forced to read material they don't care about. To counter this we offer accessible, easy to read biographies about sportspeople that will give young adults the chance to fall in love with reading.

Go to the Website Below to Join Our Community

https://mailchi.mp/7cced1339ff6/jcbcommunity

Or Find Us on Facebook at

www.facebook.com/JacksonCarterBiographies

As a Member of Our Community You Will Receive:

First Notice of Newly Published Titles

Exclusive Discounts and Offers

Influence on the Next Book Topics

Don't miss out, join today and help spread the love of reading around the world!

OTHER WORKS BY JACKSON CARTER BIOGRAPHIES

Patrick Mahomes: The Amazing Story of How Patrick Mahomes Became the MVP of the NFL

Donovan Mitchell: How Donovan Mitchell Became a Star for the Salt Lake City Jazz

Luka Doncic: The Complete Story of How Luka Doncic Became the NBA's Newest Star

The Eagle: Khabib Nurmagomedov: How Khabib Became the Top MMA Fighter and Dominated the UFC

Lamar Jackson: The Inspirational Story of How One Quarterback Redefined the Position and Became the Most Explosive Player in the NFL

Jimmy Garoppolo: The Amazing Story of How One Quarterback Climbed the Ranks to Be One of the Top Quarterbacks in the NFL

Zion Williamson: The Inspirational Story of How Zion Williamson Became the NBA's First Draft Pick

Kyler Murray: The Inspirational Story of How Kyler Murray Became the NFL's First Draft Pick

Do Your Job: The Leadership Principles that Bill Belichick and the New England Patriots Have Used to Become the Best Dynasty in the NFL

Turn Your Gaming Into a Career Through Twitch and Other Streaming Sites: How to Start, Develop and Sustain an Online Streaming Business that Makes Money

From Beginner to Pro: How to Become a Notary Public

www.ingramcontent.com/pod-product-compliance
Lightning Source LLC
LaVergne TN
LVHW051625050326
832903LV00033B/4662